Derbyshire

Charles Wildgoose

COUNTRYSIDE BOOKS

NEWBURY BERKSHIRE

First Published 2007
© Charles Wildgoose, 2007

COUNTRYSIDE BOOKS
3 Catherine Road
Newbury, Berkshire

To view our complete range of books,
please visit us at
www.countrysidebooks.co.uk

ISBN 978 1 84674 015 2

Photographs by the author
Cover picture of Chatsworth supplied by Andy Barker,
Creative Services, Sheffield City Council

Designed by Peter Davies, Nautilus Design
Produced through MRM Associates Ltd, Reading
Printed by Borcombe SP Ltd., Romsey

Contents

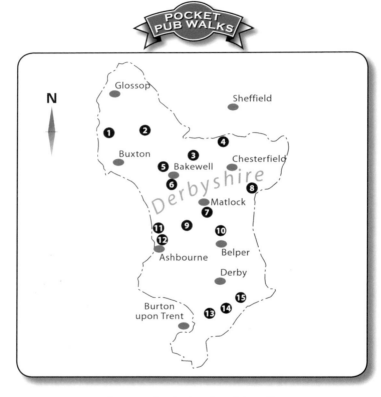

Area map showing location of the walks

Introduction

Here are fifteen circular walks dotted throughout Derbyshire in some of the finest walking country in the world, in my estimation anyway!

It's not just the stunning scenery that makes these routes special. No, it's the history and tradition of this land. It has soaked into the very ground we walk upon. Hopefully you will pick up a sense of this when you follow these circuits.

The idea is that you park at or near the pub and combine your walk with a drink and a meal. If you park in the pub car park, it should certainly be the case that you repay the landlord's hospitality and frequent his premises.

I would always advise, however, that you take a drink and a bite to eat with you in addition. If you're walking several miles and it's hot and you become thirsty, it's as well to be able to 'wet your whistle' if you need to do so.

The routes are between 2¼ and 7 miles in length, allowing plenty of choice. As regards how long they should take, I usually reckon I average 2 miles an hour. Walking speeds differ, of course, but, if you use this as the basis for working out how long you need to allow, you shouldn't be far out.

I suggest that you wear walking boots whenever you set off into the countryside. Shoes and trainers are all well and good but, if the ground is wet and muddy, you're likely to be wet and muddy, too.

My checkers have been marvellous once again – particularly Ruth, Graham and Thomas Rhodes. Ruth and Graham have walked all but two or three of the fifteen routes and I can't thank them enough. Others have done their bit, namely Kath, Elizabeth and Robert Walker as well as Carole and Stuart Middleton, Di Carnell and Julian Elliott.

Balkees is standing right behind me as I type so I mustn't forget to mention her tolerance and patience whilst I've been working on this book. She has accompanied me on all the walks and offered constructive advice (whether it's been asked for or not). Seriously, she has been wonderful.

Finally, don't forget to stand and stare – and sometimes look behind you. Enjoy the lovely scenery that you will pass through whilst using this book. It is very, very special.

Enjoy your walking.

Publisher's Note

We hope that you obtain considerable enjoyment from this book; great care has been taken in its preparation. However, changes of landlord and actual closures are sadly not uncommon. Likewise, although at the time of publication all routes followed public rights of way or permitted paths, diversion orders can be made and permissions withdrawn.

We cannot, of course, be held responsible for such diversion orders and any inaccuracies in the text which result from these or any other changes to the routes nor any damage which might result from walkers trespassing on private property. We are anxious though that all details covering the walks and pubs are kept up to date and would therefore welcome information from readers which would be relevant to future editions.

The simple sketch maps that accompany the walks in this book are based on notes made by the author whilst checking out the routes on the ground. However, for the benefit of a proper map, we do recommend that you purchase the relevant Ordnance Survey sheet covering your walk. The Ordnance Survey maps are widely available, especially through booksellers and local newsagents.

1 Whaley Bridge

The Navigation Inn

Whaley Bridge, at the southern end of the Peak Forest Canal and the northern end of the Goyt valley, is a good base to enjoy some varied walking. There are plenty of hills around, with Kinder Scout and the Pennine Way just five or six miles distant. This walk leads you to the hamlet of Taxal with its lovely old church and then you're taking in the glory of the Goyt valley. The Fernilee Reservoir marks the halfway point

Distance – 6 miles.

OS Explorer OL1 Peak District – Dark Peak area and OL24 Peak District – White Peak area. GR 012815.

The walk starts off fairly easily but becomes more testing beyond Taxal. After Fernilee Reservoir, though, it's largely 'downhill'.

Starting point The free car park at the canal wharf – the Navigation Inn doesn't have a car park.

How to get there From the A6, take the A5004 south and turn sharp left opposite the Jodrell Arms in Whaley Bridge. Continue as far as you can, passing the Navigation Inn on your right, before turning right, then right again, to reach the car park.

of the walk and was built in the late 1930s to provide water for the increasing demand in the Stockport area. The 'homeward' journey runs largely beside the River Goyt itself and is much more sheltered. 'Goyt' is a local word for a watercourse and can also be seen in more general use as 'goit'. Take some time to stand and stare now and again on this walk – there are plenty of opportunities.

THE PUB The friendly **Navigation Inn** describes itself as a 'historic pub with a modern feel'. It is certainly a hostelry that is striving to do something a little different. For instance, they have available twenty different bottled lagers from around the world. Nearer to home they always have Black Sheep Bitter on offer and guest ales such as Highgate Fury and Newman's Wolvers Ale. The food is home made and you can enjoy anything from a panini to a steak pudding or lasagne.

Whaley Bridge Walk 1

Opening times Mondays from 4 pm until 11 pm but during the rest of the week from 12 noon until 11 pm (including Sundays).
☎ 01663 719184

1 Walk back towards the railway station (next to the **Jodrell Arms**) and cross the main road. Take **Reservoir Road** immediately to the left of the station. Bear left (still on Reservoir Road) after passing under the railway bridge. Stay on this to reach **Todd**

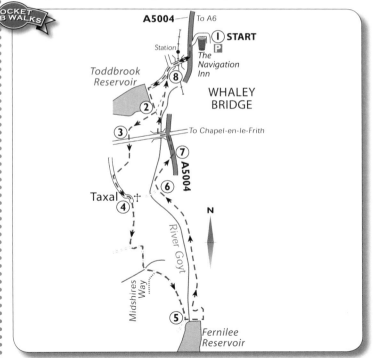

Brook Lodge (1881). Turn left immediately beyond and proceed with the reservoir on your right. The reservoir was built in 1831 and feeds water to the **Peak Forest Canal**.

2 At the end of the reservoir take the footpath on the right (along the **Midshires Way**). This path leads to a farmyard. Follow the tarmac driveway beyond it. On reaching **Mereside Gardens** on your left keep forward to the main road ahead.

3 Cross the road, taking the path to the right of the telephone box and passing **White Briars**. Keep forward, staying in the same direction up the left side of field two (with a property on your left). Follow the fenced path to a drive (with a pair of tall stone gateposts on your left). Turn right for 25 yards to the lane and turn left along it. Ignore driveways to right and left. You eventually reach **Taxal church**.

4 With the church on your left, keep forward along the lane ahead (ignoring a lane downhill immediately beyond the church). There are six bells at Taxal but in 1594 there were only three bells in the 'ryng'. Pass **Glebe Farm** on your left and stay on the lane. You're following the **Midshires Way** still. Continue on the track to pass through a gate signed 'Overton Hall Farm'. Ignore a track to the right immediately beyond the gate. Stay on the track, passing **Greenoak** on your right. Three-quarters of a mile later you reach **Overton Hall Farm** on your right. Immediately beyond join another track. Turn left downhill. Stay on the lane and descend into the valley. Cross a stream and bear left uphill. On reaching a house (**Knipe Farm**) on your left, leave the **Midshires Way**, keeping straight forward on a track with a conifer plantation on your right. This tracks runs for ½ mile, bringing you to **Fernilee Reservoir**.

5 Turn left, crossing the dam wall. Then turn left on the far side, then sharp left 50 yards later, downhill. You reach some old works. Pass these and walk along a track down the valley. The

In the Goyt valley.

track fizzles out, then follow a path. Ignore a footbridge on your left; stay on the right side of the **River Goyt**. The path then moves slightly away from the river to enter **Shallcross Wood**. Stay on the obvious path. The A5004 won't be far away to your right.

6 On reaching a stony track rising uphill from the left, cross to the path opposite, with the river still to your left. Climb a stile, continuing along the track/path in the same direction as before. This leads to a road.

7 Turn left here then left at the crossroads into **Lower Macclesfield Road**. Cross the river, turning right along **Goyt Road**. At the end of the road, head into the park and take the lower path, keeping the river on your right. Eventually the path brings you out at a converted chapel on your left.

8 Turn right at **Reservoir Road**, back to the start.

Places of interest nearby

A National Trust property, **Lyme Park** is no more than three or four miles to the west of Whaley Bridge. It has lovely gardens and grounds, which you could explore if you still have some energy left. Famously it is where Darcy emerged from the lake in the 1995 production of *Pride and Prejudice*.
☎ *01663 762023*

Or you could head south on the A6 and visit **Buxton** with its Opera House and Pavilion Gardens.

The Castle Hotel

You could spend a whole day in Castleton itself without too much difficulty – with its caverns and castle it's a fascinating place indeed. Make sure you get there early in order to park, though! Towering above the village is the Norman-built Peveril Castle – hence the name, Castleton. On this walk, you'll get good views of Winnats Pass (where a young couple were slain by three rogues many years ago as they eloped to Gretna Green) and also Mam Tor (known as the 'shivering mountain') as it looms above you. The high point of the walk will be the stretch along the ridge between Hollins Cross (watch out for the curious and greedy sheep) and Lose Hill. Then it's all downhill but still with marvellous views all around.

THE PUB

The **Castle Hotel** is on the opposite side of the road from the car park. Turn left (on foot) from the entrance to get there. It is a great English pub with oak beams and low ceilings – a combination that always appeals to me. It's well worth visiting for the ambience alone! Thwaites Lancaster Bomber, Wells Bombardier, Black Sheep Bitter and Morland Old Speckled Hen are all available – so you've got a good choice of beers. The menu is comprehensive and very tasty, with 'pub classics' such as toad in the hole, roast stuffed aubergine and chicken Monte Cristo included. Then there are fish dishes such as 'A Whale of a Fish' and Cajun swordfish steak.

Opening times All day, every day.
☎ 01433 620578

1. From the car park turn right past the **Castleton Centre**. Head along the road for **Winnats Pass**. Ignore the road to the left for **Speedwell Cavern**. Stay on the road for **Treak Cliff Cavern**.

> **Distance** – 5½ miles.
>
> **OS Explorer** OL1 Peak District – Dark Peak area. GR 149829.
>
> There's a fairly steady climb up to the ridge at Hollins Cross, with great views when you get there. The return to Castleton is easier.
>
> **Starting point** The main public pay & display car park next to the Castleton Centre in the village.
>
> **How to get there** As you drive through Castleton from the east on the A6187 the car park is on the right.

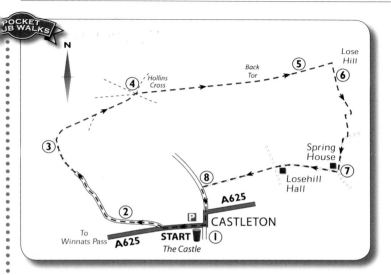

POCKET
JB WALKS

2 Rise up the road past the car park for **Speedwell Cavern** on your left. **Winnats Pass** is half left of you as you go. This dead end road rises and bears right with good views of the **Hope Valley**. Pass the entrance to **Treak Cliff Cavern**. At the bus turning area you get a good view of **Mam Tor** (the Mother Hill). Keep forward along the old tarmac road, which has suffered from subsidence.

3 Continue as far as the sharp left hand bend. Here turn right onto a track but almost immediately fork left on a path, keeping to the left of the trees. This area is **Mam Farm**. This path takes you on a steady climb to **Hollins Cross** – you should be heading generally upwards with the top of the hill above on your left. The **Hope Valley** and the cement works are to your right. After a while another path joins yours from the right. Keep heading upwards.

4 At **Hollins Cross** with its viewpoint, turn right along the ridge. The path levels out with more good views, including **Edale** to your left and **Kinder Scout** beyond. Stay on the ridge until, with

Derbyshire

The viewpoint at Hollins Cross.

the rocky outcrop of **Back Tor** directly ahead, you cross over onto the left side of the field boundary to climb up to Back Tor. There are more great views from here. Proceed along the main path along the ridge.

5 Enter the National Trust property **Lose Hill Pike** (also known as **Ward's Piece**). The flagstone path leads you to the high point of the walk. From the viewpoint bear right downhill on the flagged path.

6 Leave **Ward's Piece** by climbing a step stile. Keep forward to another stile 50 yards away. Once beyond this, turn left beside the fence on your left. After 200 yards the path bears right slightly, away from the fence, though you keep to the left of the trees. Follow the clear path beside some banking on your left. Fifty yards before a house turn sharp right (for **Hope** and **Castleton**). Pass through a wicket

gate, heading down the right side of the field beyond. Ignore a cross path as you go. On reaching a track turn right and follow it downhill. Proceed past **Castleton Service Reservoir**. The gravel track leads down to **Spring House**. Keep directly forward through this property to join a track immediately beyond.

7 Turn right for **Castleton**, following the track, with **Spring House** immediately on your right. Join another track, which rises up to a farm, but turn left here. This track subsequently runs alongside **Losehill Hall**. At a junction of tracks just beyond the Hall take the footpath directly ahead. Keep on the right side of the field. Cross the stepping stones and keep straight ahead, with **Winnats Pass** in the distance. Keep forward along a track when you reach it.

8 On reaching a T-junction, turn left along a lane leading into **Castleton**. Keep straight forward, ignoring all lanes to left and right. At the main street, turn right, back to the car.

Places of interest nearby

I would recommend a visit to **Peveril Castle.** Though a ruin, it is in a spectacular position.
☎ *01433 620613*

Then what about The Devil's Arse? Sounds lovely doesn't it? It is in fact another name for **Peak Cavern** and much more eye-catching.
☎ *01433 620285*

There are other caverns that you can explore in Castleton – **Speedwell**, **Treak Cliff** and of course **Blue John**. Castleton is the only place in the world where Blue John occurs. As I said at the beginning – you could spend the day in Castleton – and I've not even mentioned the **Castleton Centre**, where there is an information centre and museum.
☎: *01433 620679*

3 Robin Hood

The Robin Hood Inn

There's **not too much** to Robin Hood. It's a hamlet comprising a farm, a pub and one house, as far as I can see – you're in the countryside before you know it. This is not a bad thing! Most of the circuit is on the Chatsworth Estate and you follow concessionary paths that have been created by the Estate, so please respect them. If you haven't been on the hill behind Chatsworth House then you'll get a chance to see the Emperor Lake, which, by gravity alone, feeds the Emperor Fountain in the grounds of the House. According to the Chatsworth website this is 'the tallest gravity fed fountain in the world, capable of reaching 298 feet', being designed in 1843 by Joseph Paxton.

Robin Hood Walk 3

Distance – 7 miles.

OS Explorer OL24 Peak District – White Peak area.
GR 281721.

A lovely walk through beautiful Peak District scenery. Not too testing, though there is some rough ground here and there.

Starting point Park in the Birchen Edge free public car park beside the Robin Hood Inn. Get there early as there is limited space.

How to get there *The inn is at the junction of the B6050 and the A619 as it heads westward from Chesterfield to Baslow.*

THE PUB The **Robin Hood Inn** can hardly fail, situated as it is beside a Peak District car park in stunning surroundings. It is very popular with walkers and they even have their own 'end'. The beer usually comprises Riding Bitter, Banks's Bitter, Marston Pedigree and Mansfield Cask Ale. If you're feeling peckish after your walk then you will be able to tuck into items such as vegetable lasagne, broccoli, leek and Stilton bake and penne pasta. It's not an old pub but it's a comfortable, light and welcoming place.

Opening times *All day except for Mondays, when the inn opens from 11.30 am until 3 pm and 6.30 pm until 11 pm.*
☎ *01246 583186*

1 From the car park walk back to the A619 and turn right. Sixty yards later cross the road to a concessionary path on your left. Go over a stream. When the path levels, cross a track (which you will

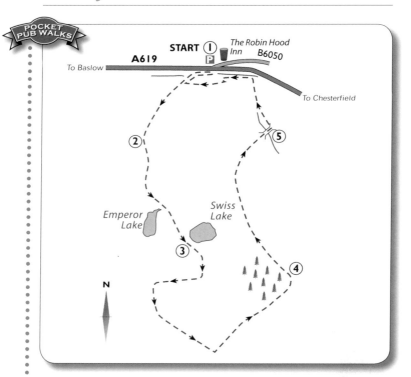

rejoin later) heading for **Beeley** via **Swiss Lake**. Cross a ladder stile, taking the path alongside a plantation on your left. You then rise up above the busy A619 in the trees below. Eventually the path leads into a field; keep forward along the right side of it. This brings you to a high step stile over a wall. Cross this and keep forward with a high wall on your left.

2 Climb another tall step stile into a plantation. Follow the path to bear right along a track. Keep forward where tracks cross. You should now be following a tarmac driveway. Ignore a concessionary path sharp right (for **Baslow**). At a crossroads of

tracks turn left. Shortly afterwards keep forward when tracks join from both sides. Then ignore a track forking right. On reaching **Emperor Lake** on your right stay on the gravel track and subsequently reach **Swiss Lake** on your left. Have a look! **Swiss Cottage** is on the far side.

3 Continue as before, ignoring the private access to **Swiss Cottage** on your left. The track gently swings right, with a farm a field away to your left. The track then swings left. Keep forward at the crossroads of tracks. A high step stile leads you out of **Chatsworth Park** and onto **Rabbit Warren Edge**. Follow the track in front as it rises. Away to your left is a plantation. When the end of it is parallel to you (to your left, and just before the top of the climb) turn left along a concessionary footpath. This will take you towards the right side of the plantation, though you soon swing slightly left. You reach a small gate near the plantation. On the far side of this, walk up the right side of a wall, with the plantation beyond the wall.

In the wood behind Chatsworth House.

Derbyshire

4 Where the wall bends left, follow the track to the left as well. **Hob Hurst's House** (an ancient burial site, not a ruined property) is to your right though and is unique as it has a square central mound in the middle. It was one of the first monuments to be taken into state care. It was excavated in 1853 by Thomas Bateman. Hob Hurst was a mythical 'elf' who haunted the nearby woods. Back on route, follow the track, with the wall on your left. It's an easy stretch, descending gently through the moorland. On reaching a stone outbuilding beyond a stone wall, swing right on the track. When the wall bends left, keep forward on the track, heading towards the A619.

5 Cross a small stone bridge before, a few yards later, turning left along a path for **Robin Hood**. Slowly descend to walk beside a brook with the road to your right. A few yards before the last pair of wooden electricity poles on the left side of the brook, turn sharp left up a path (using the steps). Bear right at the top of the steps to walk above the brook through the bracken. Then head away slightly from the brook. Cross a step stile, following the waymarked path to reach the track mentioned at the beginning. Turn sharp right to return the way you came.

Places of interest nearby

The obvious place is **Chatsworth House**. There is something for everyone at Chatsworth. It's a marvellous house with impressive gardens but don't forget it will probably be closed during the winter (though it does open before Christmas).
☎ 01246 565300

If you travel a few miles further south, then you could visit **Haddon Hall**, a very, very different prospect from Chatsworth. Haddon is a medieval manor house dating back 900 years or so.
☎ 01629 812855

4 Holmesfield

The Angel Inn

Perched on a hillside between Sheffield to the north and the Peak District to the south and west, Holmesfield is, surprisingly, one of those places that can be bypassed. It shouldn't be as it's a lovely village with some fascinating countryside nearby. It's countryside with some unusual placenames! You'll encounter some of them today as you walk along Highlightley Lane, visit Rumbling Street and pass through Johnnygate. I think they'll give you a flavour of what to expect – something a little different perhaps. It's rolling English scenery all around you, with old bridleways cutting through the fields.

THE PUB The **Angel Inn** is a pub I have no hesitation in recommending for its food and its friendly staff. They regularly have John Smith's beer available plus guests such as Ufford's Idle Hour and The Fine Ale Club's (gluten free) Against the Grain. The

Derbyshire

Distance – 4¼ miles.

OS Explorer OL24 Peak District – White Peak area. GR 320776.

This is a bit of an up and downer but nothing too testing. You'll be using ancient bridleways and there's one bit where you may have to paddle so take your walking boots! (There is an option at point 5 to avoid getting your feet wet if you prefer. The bridleway is probably more fun, though!)

Starting point In the pub car park behind the Angel Inn (parking available for customers, with the landlord's permission) or on the roadside nearby.

How to get there Holmesfield is just south of Sheffield. Take the B6054 eastward from Owler Bar on the A621.

menu is varied and mouthwatering, so you could try steamed steak and kidney pudding or 'The Angel Home-made Burger'. If you'd like something more unusual then how about pork hock braised in honey and mustard sauce?

Opening times Food is available from 12 noon until 2 pm and 6 pm until 8.30 pm every day except Sundays when it's available from 12 noon until 8 pm. The pub is closed on Mondays.
☎ 0114 2890336

[1] With your back to the **Angel** turn left along the road. Turn right along **Cartledge Lane**. Where the lane bends right (becoming **Millthorpe Lane**) keep forward along the bridle road, signed 'Brindwoodgate'. Stay on the bridle road when you reach

the entrance to **Cartledge Hall Farm**. Keep on it for the next mile or so as it winds steadily downhill. On reaching some houses ignore a footpath to the left. Keep forward to reach **Highlightley Lane**.

2 Turn right. The lane subsequently narrows between hedges. Where it widens take the footpath on your left. Walk down the left side of the field, swinging right at the bottom to a stile by a gate. Turn left over a brook to the lane.

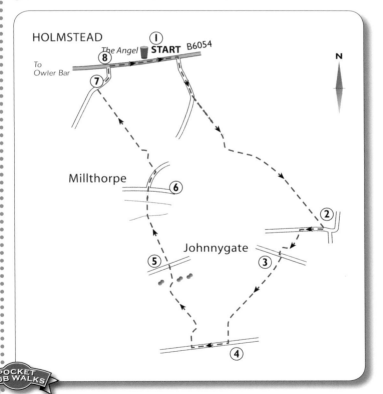

POCKET
PUB WALKS

The ford at Millthorpe.

3 Cross the lane to the path for **Rumbling Street**, a little to the left. Walk up the left side of the first four fields. In the fifth field turn right and, staying within this field, bear left uphill, with the fence/hedge on your right.

4 Turn right along the lane – this area is known as **Rumbling Street**. Immediately past the first barn on your right, turn right through the gateway and aim towards **Holmesfield**, on the skyline a couple of miles away. Stay on a track leading away from the buildings. The track leads to a wood. Where the track does a 90° right turn, keep forward on the path into the wood. Proceed to the far side, ignoring a path forking left as you go. At the edge of the wood climb the stile. Walk towards the buildings of **Johnnygate** ahead, beside a hedge on your right. At the end of the hedge, bear slightly left to a small gate. The route crosses a small paddock (past a standing stone) to reach the stile beyond.

5 Turn right on the lane for a few yards, then left on the track. Follow the bridleway if you wish to reach **Pingle Dike** – the stream in the valley bottom. Proceed on the bridleway beyond to reach a driveway leading to a property to your left. Keep forward into **Millthorpe**, crossing a ford as you go and rising up to the main road. (If you want to avoid the possibility of getting your feet wet, then, 35 yards or so after turning left off the lane and onto the track, pass through the farmgate directly ahead and walk down the left side of two fields, parallel to the bridleway immediately on your left. Cross a footbridge and continue down the left side of a third field. Cross a stile at the end of the field onto a drive. Turn right here to reach and then cross the ford to rise up to the main road beyond.)

6 Go straight across at the crossroads on the **Holmesfield** road. Some 200 yards later, on the right hand bend, take the bridleway for **Horsleygate Lane**. Stay on this for over ½ mile as it rises to the lane (ignoring a cross path and an alternative route 5 yards after the path).

7 Turn right at the lane.

8 Turn right at the main road back to the **Angel**.

Places of interest nearby

Heading into Sheffield from Owler Bar you pass through Totley to reach **Abbeydale Industrial Hamlet**, where you can step back into the past.
☎ 0114 2367731

Then there are the **Botanical Gardens** a bit further into Sheffield – there are 18 or 19 acres of gardens here and they are really worth a visit. They have recently undergone a restoration with help from the Lottery Fund.
☎ 0114 2500500

5 Monsal Head

The Stables at the Monsal Head Hotel

Monsal Head must be one of the most photographed views in the Peak District. In fact if you showed a photograph of the view to most people in the UK, the chances are that the majority would know what part of the world it is in. This short walk thoroughly explores the Monsal Head view. It's a figure of eight walk but the crossing point is some 30 yards above the valley floor, so you don't actually step on the path you've used previously. The Monsal Trail is open, where it can be, to both walkers and cyclists but originally it carried the railway line from Matlock to Buxton. I wonder whether it will ever do so again? The walk descends into the valley before you pass under the viaduct. When you return (using the Monsal Trail) you cross the viaduct and then rise back to the start, where you can enjoy a well earned drink.

THE PUB

The **Stables bar** is next to the Monsal Head Hotel. It was converted (you won't be surprised to learn) from the original stables that were here. They have retained much of their rustic charm though and some 'horsey' paraphernalia is hanging on the walls. There is also a flagstone floor and an open fireplace, which makes it very comfy on a cold winter's day. Now this is also something of a Real Ale paradise, with as many as eight beers usually on offer. The regulars include my all time favourite, Old Peculier, as well as Theakston's Best Bitter and Timothy Taylor Landlord. There are guests too, such as Whim Ales' Special Ale. Interesting dishes feature on the menu, for example grilled barramundi, and boneless quail, potato and onion pancake.

Opening times All day from 11.30 am until 11 pm except Sundays, when it's 12 noon until 10.30 pm. Food is served from 12 noon until 9 or 9.30 pm.
☎ 01629 640250

Distance –2¼ miles.

OS Explorer OL24 Peak District – White Peak area. GR 84715.

With good views and marvellous scenery, don't be lulled into thinking this short walk is a doddle – there's some uphill movement required at times!

Starting point Behind the Monsal Head Hotel in the district council pay & display car park.

How to get there Monsal Head is a couple of miles north-west of Ashford in the Water on the B6465.

Derbyshire

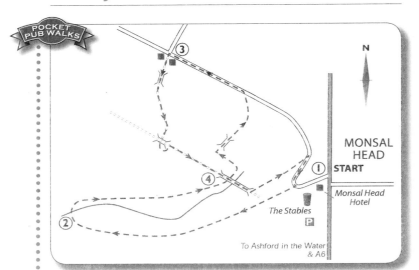

1. Standing with your back to the front of the **Monsal Head Hotel**, walk left to the **Monsal View Café**. In front of this is a marvellous view with the viaduct below. Take the path for **Ashford** and **Monsal Dale**. After 10 or 12 yards the path forks; take the lower one. The path levels out before descending to the **River Wye**. Keep beside this until you reach and cross a footbridge.

2. Turn right upstream beyond the bridge. You pass a weir on your right before eventually coming out, with the viaduct ahead of you. Pass through a stile by a gate beneath the viaduct. Follow the path underneath it. This wheels left, with the river on your right, to bring you to a footbridge. Cross the river for the second time. You reach **Netherdale Farm**. Keep left of the buildings and then swing left on the drive to the road. Turn left along the road for 500 yards.

3. On reaching the crossroads, turn left, back to the river (look out for the trout as you cross it!). Bear left up the old lane and stay on

The view from Monsal Head.

it under the **Monsal Trail**. Turn right onto the Trail and keep right along it so that you're walking with the river down below to your left. You pass the remains of **Monsal Dale Station**. Eventually you reach the viaduct and cross it.

4 Keep forward towards the large metal doors that block the tunnel. Just before it turn left up a path and keep going to reach a T-junction of paths. Turn right up here back to the **Monsal Head Hotel**.

Places of interest nearby

How about heading a few miles south-east to **Bakewell**? You could have a walk around the shops and beside the River Wye before having tea, and make sure you eat a Bakewell pudding! You could also have a look around the Old House Museum (☎ *01629 813642*).

The Lathkil Hotel

With the **Lathkil Hotel in Over Haddon** sitting proudly above Lathkill Dale (yes, they're spelt differently) you have another marvellously positioned pub in the Peak District. Sit in the window at the Lathkil Hotel and enjoy that view – preferably when the sun isn't shining too strongly. Over Haddon is where the Wildgooses lived in the 19th century and earlier – so that's one claim to fame for the area! Seriously though, Over Haddon is one of those attractive Peak District limestone villages perched on high ground overlooking a dale. The walk starts off along a quietish lane, then you experience a truly stunning view of Lathkill Dale itself before walking down the dale to return to the pub. On the way you can go underground and see something a little different – but more of that later.

Distance – 4¾ miles.

OS Explorer OL24 Peak District – White Peak area.
GR 207664 (pub).

A fairly moderate walk with a steep descent halfway round and an ascent at the end. In between there's some undemanding walking, though you may have to watch your step a little in the dale. **Please note: you will not be able to walk this route on a Wednesday between October and January as a concessionary path in Lathkill Dale is closed.**

Starting point There's not much space near the pub at the eastern end of the village. Use the district council pay & display car park at the western end (GR 203664).

How to get there Take the B5055 south-west from Bakewell before turning left a mile outside Bakewell for Over Haddon. Follow the signs in the village for the car park.

THE PUB

The **Lathkil Hotel** occupies a prime Peakland spot and what a delight it is to make use of it after a challenging walk. There's no doubt that it's another good Real Ale pub, with regulars such as Thornbridge Brewery's Lord Marples and Whim Ales' Hartington Bitter available. Then there are guests such as Belvoir Brewery's Sky Hopper and the Anglo Dutch Brewery's Devil's Knell. There's usually a buffet in the restaurant every day where you can enjoy a steak and kidney pie or minty lamb casserole (or even venison, mushroom and red wine casserole).

Opening times Monday to Friday 11.30 am until 3 pm and then 6.30 pm until 11 pm. Weekends all day.
☎ *01629 812501*

Derbyshire

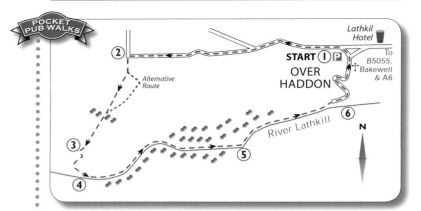

1. Turn left out of the car park entrance, then left again at the T-junction (along **Monyash Road**). Stay on this lane for nearly a mile. Where the road forks, go left along the minor lane. Nearly another mile later, at the right hand 90 degrees bend, turn left along the drive for **Haddon Grove Farm**.

2. The footpath goes right through the farmyard (though the present owner is quite happy for walkers to follow the track to the left and pass through the campsite). To follow the public footpath though, keep straight forward on reaching the far end of the farmhouse and leave the farmyard at the far end by a track through a gateway. This takes you down the right side of a breeze-block building. Keep forward to pass through a squeezer stile in the line of trees. Leave the trees 4 or 5 yards later by another stile. Head forward through the field ahead, 15 yards from a wall on your right. Beyond the valley ahead is **One Ash Grange** – for 200 years between the 1690s and the 1890s this was the home of the Bowman family, who were Quakers. Pass through a gap and gently descend.

3. Pass through a wooden kissing gate to enter English Nature's **Derbyshire Dales National Nature Reserve**. There are fine

views from here – it's a place where a stop is justly deserved. Zigzag down the path into **Lathkill Dale** itself.

4 Turn left along the path in the valley bottom and head downstream. The **River Lathkill** is one of the cleanest and clearest of rivers – assuming it is running. During the summer it dries up, with any water disappearing underground. Pass through a gate into **Palmerston Wood** – this concessionary path is closed on a Wednesday between October and January. It is nice and shady in hot weather. Eventually, look out for a bridge on your right. Cross this to **Bateman's House**. Do take the opportunity to climb down the metal ladder and wind the dynamo. Then look at the water below. You will feel cold down here even though you're only a few feet below ground.

5 Pass though a couple of gateposts to come out in the open but, just before you do, 10 yards before the gateposts look out on your right for the sough (pronounced 'suff'), from which water runs out of the old leadmine nearby.

6 Eventually you reach **Lathkill** Lodge. Head up the lane to the left of it. Zigzag all the way back up to the car.

Places of interest nearby

Three or four miles east of Over Haddon is **Rowsley** (pronounced with an 'o' as in rowing boat). Here you can visit **Caudwell's Mill** and explore this historic flour mill. There's also a shop here and the Country Parlour, where you can enjoy a refreshing cup of coffee (and perhaps one of their generous slices of cake) as you listen to the waters of the millrace tumble past the window.
☎ 01629 734374

7 Matlock Bath

The Midland Hotel

Matlock Bath is a very popular tourist attraction. Visit it on a Sunday and you'll see what I mean. (That reminds me – you should get there early on a Sunday if you want to find a parking space!) There are gift shops, there are chip shops, there are all sorts of tourist attractions here. The popularity of Matlock Bath probably originates with the warm springs discovered as long ago as the end of the 17th century.

In Victorian times its reputation grew. The walk takes you away from the crowds and you will be surprised how very few of the visitors you'll see whilst on your walk. The route climbs up to High Tor, where, if you're brave enough, you can stare down over 100 yards to the river below. The walk finishes along a lovely woodland path which brings you back into Matlock Bath.

THE PUB

The **Midland Hotel** nestles in a bend of the River Derwent, a lovely spot for a beer garden. This is one of the few places I know where they cut *down* on the choice of food they cook during the summer – all because it gets so busy. There will still be plenty of food in summer, just not as much as in winter. Try their chicken tikka, crispy coated fish medley or gammon steak. Regular beers are usually John Smith's and Peak Ale's Bakewell Best Bitter but there are guests such as Peakstone's Black Hole. Try and sit in the beer garden in the sunshine and watch the river flow.

Distance – 2¾ miles.

OS Explorer OL24 Peak District – White Peak area. GR 297583.

A lovely walk with simply splendid views of the Derwent Valley. Why Matlock and Matlock Bath aren't in the Peak District I'll never know. Be prepared for a couple of climbs.

Starting point Matlock Bath railway station pay & display car park.

How to get there Head south on the A6 from Matlock. Turn left in front of the Midland Hotel to park in the station car park.

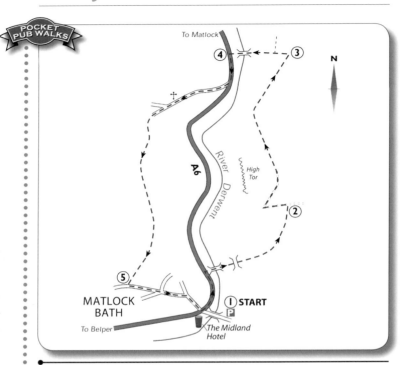

Opening times *In summer it's open all day from 12 noon until 11 pm; in winter from 12 noon until 3 pm (and then open again in the evening).*
☎ *01629 582630*

1 From the car park, walk back to the A6. Turn right, with the **Midland Hotel** on your left, then 250 yards later turn right across a footbridge. Pass under the railway bridge and there (on your left) is the cable car station. Go through the stile to the right of the entrance and walk up the tarmac path beyond. Ignore a couple of paths to the right. You then reach some houses.

2 Turn left along the track beyond house number 13. Enter the **High Tor Grounds**. Follow the tarmac track as it swings right and then left. Ignore the left fork to a mast. A marvellous view of **Matlock** opens out on your right. As the track levels you should bear right along a stony track. If you wish though, keep forward and rise up to 'enjoy' the view from **High Tor**, but TAKE CARE – there is no fencing and a 350 ft drop to the **River Derwent** below. Returning to the route, keep on down the path and make use of the two viewpoints as you descend.

3 Eventually you reach another entrance to the Grounds. Turn left here downhill. Continue and pass under the railway line (ignoring a path to the right as you go). Keep forward across the footbridge to reach the A6.

Stunning views are to be seen on this walk.

Derbyshire

4 Cross the A6 with care, and turn left on the far side. Some 100 yards later, fork right, up **St John's Road**. This leads uphill and you should ignore a lane to the left so that you reach **St John's Chapel** above you on your right. Beyond this, fork left along a track, Public Footpath no 69, to **Matlock Bath**. The rusty cable on your left is supposed to have pulled the trams that ran in Matlock at the end of the 19th century. At the farm entrance, fork left along the footpath through the trees. This path is easy to follow and you can't get lost! After you've passed under the cable car and over an access drive to the **Heights of Abraham** you descend to a road.

5 Turn left here. Pass **Masson Cottage** (dated 1771) to reach the octagonal toll cottage. Ignore the road turning sharp right here and also ignore **Masson Road** to the left. Keep on down the road ahead to subsequently bear right to descend **Upperwood Road** and reach the **Midland Hotel** again. Cross the road (the A6), using the pelican crossing to your right, to get back to your car.

Places of interest nearby

Take your pick in Matlock Bath. If you've got young children with you then there's **Gulliver's Kingdom.**
☎ *01925 444888*
If you're interested in lead mining history then there's the **Peak District Mining Museum**.
☎ *01629 583834*
Or you could have a cable car ride up to the **Heights of Abraham** and follow a guide into one of their underground showcaves.
☎ *01629 582365*

8 Hardwick Hall

The Hardwick Inn

The countryside around Hardwick Hall has undergone something of a regeneration, at least as regards walking, in these last few years. With the opening up of the Teversal and Rowthorne Trails the opportunities to create lovely circular walks has greatly increased. In addition the National Trust has also provided a few more concessionary paths in the grounds of the Hall. Hopefully this walk takes advantage of at least some of the opportunities. It is a fairly gentle circuit with some excellent scenery in an area that many walkers wouldn't dream of visiting – more fool them. This is a really fascinating region to explore.

Distance – 5¾ miles.

OS Explorer 269 Chesterfield & Alfreton. GR 458633.

A fairly level and easy walk, the only climb being at the start. After that it's mainly on level ground.

Starting point The Hardwick Inn. Customers can park in the pub car park, with the landlord's permission. If possible, park in the overflow car park.

How to get there From junction 29 of the M1 take the exit signed 'Hardwick Hall'. Then take the first left (also signed 'Hardwick Hall') and ignore the next sign for the Hall. Stay on the lane you're on for over 2 miles before bearing left at the staggered crossroads.

THE PUB
The **Hardwick Inn** is a great pub. The menu is extensive and includes hot main courses from the grill, such as 8oz fillet steak or 12oz rib eye steak. There are Hardwick Estate lamb dishes like shepherd's pie and lamb steak and they also make some lovely sandwiches. We can especially recommend the local oak roast smoked salmon! The regular beers are Morland Old Speckled Hen, Theakston's XB, Ruddles County and Marston's Pedigree. It's a historic pub dating back 500 or 600 years and well worth searching out. It is very popular and gets extremely busy, though they always seem to cope with the crowds of people who use it.

Opening times The pub is open all day every day. Bar meals are available from 11.30 am until 9.30 pm on Monday to Saturday and from 12 noon until 9 pm on Sunday.
☎ *01246 850245*

1 With your back to the **Hardwick Inn** turn right up the driveway between the gateposts (signed 'No Entry'). Proceed up the access road, with the old Hall above and half left of you. As you negotiate a tight left hand bend, pass through the small bridlegate beside a farmgate on your right. Walk along the grassy track beyond towards the gate on the opposite side of the field. Climb the stile here and follow the path uphill. Where it levels out bear right, ignoring the path to the left. Walk beneath the trees in **Lady Spencer's Wood** – you will leave Derbyshire and enter Nottinghamshire about halfway through. Towards the end of the wood, descend the steps and (ignoring another path to the left) continue forward to the corner of the wood.

2 Cross a stile and turn left along the lane. Pass the buildings at **Norwood** and continue beyond them. Half a mile after Norwood, immediately after crossing a road bridge, turn left onto the **Teversal Trail**.

3 Walk along this for ¾ mile, re-entering Derbyshire as you do so. Turn left through a squeezer stile to join the **Rowthorne Trail**.

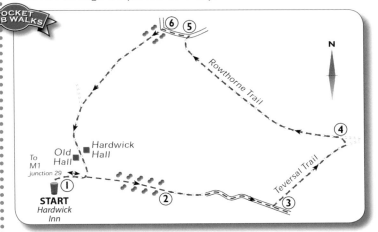

4 Turn left along the Trail and stay on it for about 1½ miles to reach a car park. Turn right to reach the lane.

5 Turn left along the lane for 400 yards.

6 At a small grass triangle, turn left towards the grounds of **Hardwick Hall**. Pass a lodge on your right to enter the estate. Keep forward on the tarmac access road, ignoring another access

The 'new' Hardwick Hall.

road joining the one you're on from the right. Keep forward to pass between **Hardwick Hall** itself (on your left) and the **Old Hall** (on your right). Beyond the Old Hall, at the end of a high wall and with **The Stableyard** to your left, keep forward downhill, passing the **Stone Centre** on your left and then bearing right downhill, back to the **Hardwick Inn**.

Places of interest nearby

I can thoroughly recommend **Hardwick Hall and gardens** for a visit. I'm a member of the National Trust and I regularly pop in just to walk round the garden and *sometimes* take the odd cream tea. The Hall is a marvellous building – created by Bess of Hardwick, with her initials 'ES' standing boldly on top. What a woman she must have been, especially for those days.
☎ *01246 850430*

9 Carsington

The Miners Arms

Since the building of the Carsington Water dam there's
no doubt that this region has become more popular with
walkers and other visitors. That's great, because the area
is really interesting with some attractive scenery. By the time
you've got to the top of the hill near the start of the walk you
will have the opportunity to enjoy a marvellous view across
Carsington Water. It is a focal point that draws people to it.
Carsington Pasture is riddled with mineshafts (most of them

capped) so don't go jumping on any depressions in the ground. These earthworks, though, give you some idea as to how man has plundered the good earth hereabouts for his own gain, for the lead that lies below ground – and they've been doing it since Roman times.

THE PUB The **Miners Arms** provides a wide range of food. There is a carvery on a Sunday that comprises roast pork, beef and turkey whilst the other dishes could be a lamb in garlic casserole, tuna steak with a sweet chilli dip or steak pie. Grills and baguettes are on offer too – hopefully something to suit every taste. Beers are usually supplied by one of the small local breweries, Peak Ales and Thornbridge Brewery, plus a guest beer such as Fuller's London Pride. It's a child friendly pub with a good sized beer garden.

Distance – 4¾ miles.

OS Explorer OL24 Peak District – White Peak area. GR 253533.

The early part of the circuit involves a steep climb up out of Carsington village. After that the walk is much easier with no further ascents.

Starting point The car park of the Miners Arms (parking available for customers, with the landlord's permission) or on the road just behind the pub.

How to get there Carsington village is at the northern tip of Carsington Water and reached from the B5035 between Wirksworth and Ashbourne. As you travel through the village the pub is on the south side of the road.

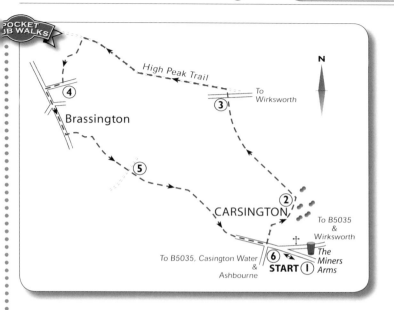

POCKET
PUB WALKS

High Peak Trail

N

④

Brassington

③   To Wirksworth

⑤

②

CARSINGTON

To B5035 & Wirksworth

The Miners Arms

To B5035, Casington Water & Ashbourne

⑥

START ①

Opening times *Monday to Friday from 11 am to 3 pm and 7 pm to 11 pm; Saturday 11 am to 3 pm and 6 pm to 11 pm; Sunday open all day until 11 pm.*
☎ *01629 540207*

---

1 Turn right from the car park entrance behind the pub. Pass the small triangular village green on your right and the stump of the Saxon preaching cross. At the main road keep forward towards the sharp left hand bend. Get on the right side of the road. Turn right up the track between houses. Continue as far as you can, eventually going up some steps to reach the last cottage and keeping immediately to the right of it to reach a field. Climb up this steep hillside, generally heading slightly right as you go – you need to be drifting towards the wood.

2 On reaching the top right hand corner of the field (with the wood immediately to your right) you reach a stile. Don't pass through this; turn left to walk alongside the wall, keeping it on your right. This large field is **Carsington Pastures** and there is much evidence of the leadmining that has taken place here in the past. Keep the wall beside you on your right as it bends right. Pass the remains of a windmill as you proceed.

3 You reach a road. Cross this, looking out for cars. Keep forward across a narrow field to reach the **High Peak Trail**. Turn left along the Trail. Ignore the footpath crossing the Trail after ½ mile. **Harboro Rocks** is on your right here. Another ½ mile later, just beyond a cutting, take the path to your left, signed '**Limestone Way**' and '**Brassington**'. Continue along the left side of the field beyond, moving slightly away from the wall to pass through a gateway. Stay in the same direction in the second field. Bear right in the third field along the grassy track to your right. This track then bears left. Keep forward into the field, aiming for the far left corner and the buildings there. Pass through the stile into the farmyard and follow the drive away from the farm.

4 Turn right at the road. Then turn left at the T-junction, down towards **Brassington**. Stay on the main road into the village. Ignore all roads to right and left. At a point where the road is quite steep and there's a road turning sharp right, take the footpath on your left for **Carsington**. Keep forward to reach a stile on your right leading into the field beyond. Cross to the stile opposite, keeping in the same direction in the second field. In the third field turn left beside the wall on your left. Turn right in field four, beside the wall on your right. Enter field five, following the path between the old lead workings and shafts. The path then descends to follow a track to a stile.

5 Cross the walled track. Follow the path to the far right corner of the first field. In the second field keep to the left of the small

A stile complete with boundary post.

outcrop of rocks. In the third field the path levels out and you cross a fallen wall by a redundant stile (just in front of an old pond). Beyond the redundant stile bear slightly right before starting to descend to a stile by a double gate. An excellent view of **Carsington Water** comes into sight as you go. Cross the stile by the double gate and continue on the path. It soon becomes a track. Cross another stile and descend into **Carsington village**.

6 At the road keep forward and you will soon reach the pub.

Places of interest nearby

At **Carsington Water**, there is the opportunity to see the birdlife on the reservoir, using one of the four hides. There's also a picnic area, the chance to hire a bike and go for a ride, or even undertake another walk if you fancy it. You can top this off with a visit to the restaurant, café or kiosk and a bit of shopping. To get to Carsington Water from the pub, return to the B5035 and turn right. A mile or two later, just beyond the Knockerdown pub, turn left for Carsington Water.
☎ *01629 540696*

10 Ambergate

The Hurt Arms

This walk passes through a couple of very different areas. Firstly, the lovely woodland of Shining Cliff Woods and then a stretch beside the Cromford Canal. In Shining Cliff Woods, a Site of Special Scientific Interest, there is an old yew tree that is supposed to have been the home of one Betty Kenny in the 17th century and to have provided the inspiration for the nursery rhyme *Rock a Bye Baby*. You will see the Betty Kenny Trail signposted and this leads to the yew – a walk for another day perhaps. The second half of the route runs alongside the Cromford Canal and is usually full of interest and wildlife, especially in spring and summer, so take your binoculars. Even the odd pike used to be seen in the water – keep your eyes peeled.

Derbyshire

Distance – 5½ miles.

OS Explorer OL24 Peak District – White Peak area. GR 348516.

A moderate route with just one climb after the section through the woods. Then there's a steeper descent to the A6, with a level walk back to the pub.

Starting point The car park at the Hurt Arms (parking available for customers, with the landlord's permission).

How to get there Ambergate is on the A6 between Matlock and Derby, and the pub is situated at the junction with the A610. You can't miss it!

THE PUB The **Hurt Arms** stands at the junction with the road to Ripley, a large stone detached building beside the A6. It's a nice pub and bills itself as the 'Home of Derbyshire Ballooning'; so you could perhaps book for a hot air balloon ride after your walk! The regular beers are Courage Directors and Ruddles County, with guests such as Everards Tiger. Lots of choice, foodwise, with toasted sandwiches, main courses (liver and onions, gammon steak and sirloin steak included) and warm baguettes (beef, ham and tuna). It's a pleasant place to relax after the walk.

Opening times 11 am to 11 pm every day except Sunday when it's 12 noon until 10.30 pm.
☎ *01773 852006*

[1] From the car park of the **Hurt Arms** return to the A6 and turn right. After 200 yards turn right into **Holly Lane** and continue for 250 yards Just beyond the **River Derwent** take the track

on the right. This is well signed and includes a reference to the **Betty Kenny Trail**. On your left is **The Birches**, a Woodland Trust wood. Keep on the track. Some 400 yards later, by a garage, a number of paths converge – keep right, taking the lower path (still on the **Betty Kenny Trail**).

2 You reach an old industrial site. Continue through this with buildings on either side. On reaching a couple of impressive stone gateposts, keep right of them. Immediately beyond the old works ignore the path to the left to the **Youth Hostel**. A little bit further along keep forward across a track to enter **Shining Cliff**

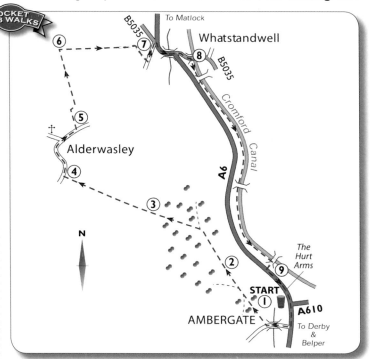

The Cromford Canal.

Woods, owned by the Forestry Commission. Over to your right you will hear cars on the A6. The path starts to rise gently. After 120 yards or so, ignore a path to the left; keep forward on the level path. At the next fork in the path, fork left for **Alderwasley** and **Whatstandwell**. Follow this, rising gently, for 500 yards.

3 Leave the woods by climbing the stile. Keep forward along the grassy path beyond. Then the path starts to rise. Pass through a kissing gate. Keep 40 yards left of the playing field. Cross another stile to reach a track. Follow this to the right. Pass a war memorial, a cross on a cairn. As the track descends, to your right is the partly whitewashed **Alderwasley Hall** with **Crich Stand** to its right in the distance.

4 On reaching the road, turn right. Pass the entrance to **Alderwasley Hall School** as you then rise on the road and bear right. Ignore **Chapel Hill** on your left and continue on **New Road** (following the **Midshires Way**).

5 After 250 yards, turn left along a track (still on the **Midshires Way**). At the far end of the track, turn right towards the stile at the bottom of the field. Turn left in the second field. Head up the right side of the third field to the top right corner. Pass through the stile here and turn right immediately, towards **Crich Stand**.

6 Head down the right side of the next four fields to reach a house in the bottom right corner of the fourth field. Walk down the path beside the house, then the path to the right of the driveway. Follow the drive for a few yards until it bends right. Cross it here and pick up the path beyond. You reach a road.

7 Cross this and follow the path down the right side of the field beyond to the A6. Cross the bridge over the **Derwent**, with care. As the A6 bends right keep forward up the hill, signed for **Crich** and **South Wingfield**.

8 Turn right after 50 or 60 yards, alongside the **Cromford Canal**. With the canal on your left continue for the next couple of miles. After the first house on your right though, look over the wall – the house is built on a railway tunnel. As you come towards the end of the 2 miles beside the canal you pass under a bridge; to your left, on the other side of the canal, is a large detached brick house – continue along the canal beyond this. Immediately before the next bridge fork right (following the **Derwent Valley Heritage Way**). The track brings you back to the A6.

9 Turn left back to the start.

Places of interest nearby

Crich Tramway Museum is just a couple of miles north of the Hurt Arms. Whether you're particularly interested in trams or just fancy a ride on one, then a visit to this fascinating collection could be an ideal way to finish off your day in this part of Derbyshire.
☎ *01773 854321*
If you've still got some energy, you could even walk up to **Crich Stand** next door and admire the view.

11 Thorpe

The Dog & Partridge

This walk takes you through probably the most spectacular scenery you'll see in Derbyshire. OK, it's arguable, but it's certainly some of the best, especially on the first half of the walk as you descend into Dovedale and then walk up the dale itself. This is the world of Izaak Walton (of *Compleat Angler* fame). On the second part of the circuit you have the chance to get away from other people and reflect a little as you head back to your starting point at the Dog and Partridge. Ideally you might want to be walking through Dovedale before the crowds are there, so why not make an early start?

Distance – 6¾ miles.

OS Explorer OL24 Peak District – White Peak area.
GR 163504.

A fairly strenuous walk with one descent early on and then
an ascent just after the halfway mark. **Please note:** If the
River Dove should be flooded and the stepping stones
under water, it will be necessary to retrace your steps from
point 4.

Starting point Narlows Lane free car park near the Dog
& Partridge (or in the pub car park if you are a customer).
The walk is described from the public car park.

How to get there Take the A515 between Ashbourne and
Buxton. At the crossroads, with the turn to Tissington going
west, turn off eastwards. Just over a mile later you'll reach the
Dog and Partridge.

THE PUB The **Dog & Partridge** has always been a popular pub with
walkers and visitors. Marston's Pedigree, Black Sheep Bitter
and Worthington Classic are usually available and there's a
good choice of food, with sandwiches, hot baguettes and jacket
potatoes as well as fish, meat and vegetarian dishes available.
This pub is ideally sited, being on the way into Dovedale.

Opening times 12 noon to 3 pm and 6 pm to 11 pm every
day.
☎ 01335 350235

1 From the car park, walk to the **Dog & Partridge**. Follow the road
to **Thorpe** to the right of it. Stay on this as it descends and bears

left into the village. Take the second left (**Hall Lane**) towards **Thorpe church**.

2 Turn right at the grass triangle along **Digmire Lane**. Where the road bends right, follow the path in the corner. Keep forward through three fields to reach a bungalow. Keep right of this and cross the yard, passing through a stile by a gate, then another gate 15 yards later. Head through the middle of the field ahead to slowly descend. On reaching a small gate, pass through. There is a marvellous view of **Ilam** at the far end of the valley. Descend just to the right of the buildings at the bottom of the hill.

3 Turn left along the road. Immediately before the first roadbridge, turn right into the fields. Follow the path through three fields, entering woodland in the third. The **River Dove** will be on your left and eventually you reach a fourth field. At the far side of this, cross the footbridge over the river.

4 Turn right along the track beyond, walking up the left side of the river to reach the stepping stones. (If you are unlucky and they are flooded, I'm afraid there is no alternative but to retrace your steps to the start.) To continue the walk, turn left beyond the stepping stones, following the river (now on your left) for the next couple of miles. As you go, you pass the limestone outcrops of **Tissington Spires**. Ignore any minor paths. Look out too for the limestone archway of **Reynard's Cave**, above to your right. **Ilam Rock** is the next notable feature, on the other side of the river in Staffordshire. After the path bears round to the right and uphill, you reach a couple of caves known as **Doveholes**.

5 Some 40 yards later turn right up a narrower path, signed for **Alsop-en-le-Dale**, 1¾ miles away. A climb ensues! After a good ½ mile you come out in the open, with **Hanson Grange** to your left (with its stoned-up windows). Keep forward for 60 yards before turning right towards the walled copse of trees at the end of the field. Keep to the right of the copse, crossing a stile in the

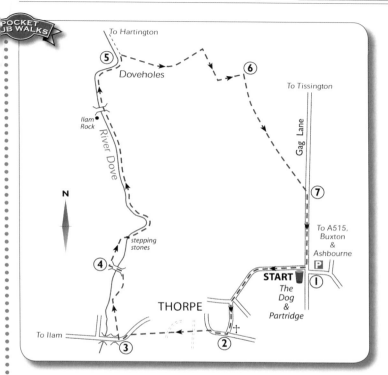

field corner. Keep forward on the right side of the wall ahead. In the field corner, climb a stile, turning left as you do so to walk up the left side of a wall rising ahead. Keep forward, crossing another stile, and with the wall, then the buildings, on your right, you reach a concrete drive.

6 Turn right into the farmyard, keeping all buildings on your right. At the far end of the farmyard, cross a stile immediately left of two farmgates. Keep alongside the wall on your right in field 1. Keep forward across fields 2 and 3, though partway through field 3, bear slightly left. Keep forward in fields 4, 5 and 6 before walking down the right side of field 7. In field 8 bear slightly left, towards the stile at the bottom of the field. Bear slightly left in field 9, cutting the corner of field 10 to reach a track. Turn left here for **Gag Lane**.

7 Turn right along the narrow lane. A mile later you arrive back at the car park.

Places of interest nearby

Travel south down to **Ashbourne** (the home of Shrovetide Football) and have a look round this attractive market town. The parish church of St Oswald's (with a spire over 200 feet high) is worth exploring. You may also wish to arrange a visit to watch the Shrovetide football. It's a game that can last two days and is not for the faint hearted. It seems to have few rules and involves the Up'ards playing the Down'ards. When you learn that the goals are three miles apart you can see that it is a bit different. It takes place on Shrove Tuesday and Ash Wednesday and apparently originated centuries ago. If I had to describe it I'd say it's like a giant rugby scrum played by a crowd rather than a team.

Looking towards Ilam.

12 **Mappleton**

The Okeover Arms

The first part of the walk, in Derbyshire, is along a stretch of the River Dove that isn't so well walked by the public. This is surprising, as the scenery is gorgeous. You then cross the river into Staffordshire and climb up to the village of Blore with its fascinating church, which is well worth a visit if only for the Bassett alabaster tomb. Then you walk through the fields above the Dove before descending past Okeover Hall and heading back to the Okeover Arms at Mappleton (or Mapleton, as spelt on some maps!). This is a splendid part of the country.

Distance – 5¼ miles.

OS Explorer 259 Derby. GR 165480.

Probably one of my favourite walks in the book. It's a moderate sort of route with just one climb (up to Blore) and one descent.

Starting point You can either park on the road near the church or in the pub car park (though please ask permission).

How to get there Mappleton is 1½ miles north-west of Ashbourne between the A52 Leek road and the A515 Buxton road.

THE PUB At the end of the 19th century the **Okeover Arms** used to be the Okeover Temperance Hotel! There's a photograph of it in the pub. Fortunately you can now get a pint of beer. They are all guests, so they change regularly. You may be able to try Timothy Taylor Landlord, A Bit of Fresh from Tower Brewery or Wells Bombardier – it depends what's on. There is also a good choice of food available, such as roast topside of beef, roast leg of Derbyshire lamb and stir fried duck breast with a hoi sin sauce.

Opening times In summer, all day, every day. In winter, 12 noon to 3 pm and 6 pm to 11 pm.
☎ 01335 350305

1 Take the path opposite the **Okeover Arms**, walking to the far right corner of the field. Cross the road. Follow the footpath opposite. In the first two fields the path runs beside the **River Dove** on your left. It then cuts across the middle of the third field

to the gate opposite. Continue upriver for about a mile. With **Dove Cottage** ahead of you, walk up the left side of a fence to reach the cottage. Pass through a stile beside a redbrick building. Follow the track beyond all the way to **Coldwall Bridge**.

2 Turn left on the **Limestone Way**. This runs from **Castleton** to **Rocester**. Look upstream from the bridge towards **Bunster Hill**. Climb up the hillside beyond the bridge on a track running directly away from the bridge towards the highest tree ahead. From there the track swings left, but look at the view behind you as you go. Pass through a gateway and walk through **Coldwall Farm**, leaving it by the driveway.

3 On reaching a lane, turn right for 450 yards into **Blore**. On the left is **Blore Hall**. Subsequently turn left at the crossroads.

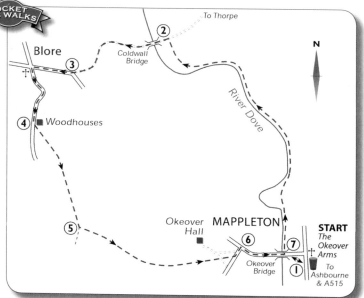

St Mary's church, Mappleton.

Almost immediately you reach the church. Do visit it, as there is a marvellous memorial to the Bassett family inside, as well as some other memorials that merit a second look. Continue on the single track lane you were on before as it descends, then rises.

4 On reaching **Woodhouses** on your left, bear slightly left off the road, alongside a long, low, stone building on your left. Pass through the left hand of two gates. Follow the walled path

beyond to reach a stone outbuilding on your left. Continue on the walled track and then on the top side of the next three fields. At the end of the third field, pass through a gate. There is a property on your right. Pass a water trough on your right and then go through another gate into the farmyard. Keep forward on a track, as though to pass between a barn on your left and a brick building on your right.

5 In front of the stone barn though, turn left through a gate. Head downhill with a wall on your right. Cross a stile and make for the corner of a hedge ahead on your right. At the hedge corner, bear very slightly right, towards the far end of a wall on your right, where there is some fencing. Clamber over the ladder stile here. Continue in the same direction, keeping to the right of a stone building ahead. Climb the stile beside the gate beyond this building. Follow a grassy track, heading downhill. Follow the track through the trees of **Okeover Park** to reach a driveway to **Okeover Hall** (the Hall being to your left). Cross the driveway to reach a tarmac road. Turn left here to another road.

6 At the T-junction turn right to cross **Okeover Bridge**.

7 At the far side of the bridge follow the path on your right, back to the **Okeover Arms**.

Places of interest nearby

I'm almost tempted to say **Alton Towers** but I rather suspect that my suggestion would not prove popular after a walk. So how about travelling down the road towards Ashbourne and enjoying a short bike ride along the **Tissington Trail** It's probably the best way to use the Trail and you may discover you've got muscles you've forgotten about.
☎ *01335 343156 for details.*

13 Milton

The Swan Inn

This area was part of ancient **Mercia**, in fact nearby Repton was its capital. I dare say 1100 years or so ago it may have been the sort of place where you wouldn't want to be seen dead – otherwise you might have been. The end of the 9th century was when marauding Vikings came knocking on the door of the Anglo Saxons, murdering and plundering (allegedly). It's much quieter now, thank goodness. These bridleways you walk on, though, are likely to have been the same routes used by the ancient Angles, Saxons and Vikings. It's a sobering thought.

Distance – 3¾ miles.

OS Explorer 245 The National Forest. GR 320263.

Probably one of the easiest walks in the book. Hardly any slopes to speak of and in a lovely underwalked area. It might be muddy here and there.

Starting point On the road near the Swan Inn (or ask permission if you want to park in the pub car park).

How to get there As you enter Repton from the A38 (via Willington) turn left at the cross and follow the road into Milton. In the village turn right to the Swan.

Bear this in mind as you come back towards Milton village along the, sometimes rather vague, bridleway.

THE PUB It's always nice to get a good welcome in a pub and that's what we got when we visited the **Swan Inn**. They always have Marston's Pedigree on tap as well as a seasonal guest such as Christmas Ale. Food is available at lunchtime on Friday, Saturday and Sunday, when you can try their bar snacks, sandwiches, jacket potatoes and baguettes. The evening menu is more extensive – oh, and it's best to book for Sunday lunchtime. They don't do junk food here, it's 99% home made. At present you can even take your own sandwiches if you have a drink there – best to give them a ring to check though.

Opening times *Monday to Thursday 6 pm to 11 pm only; Friday 12 noon to 2 pm and 6 pm to 11 pm; Saturday 12 noon to 3 pm and 7 pm to 11 pm; Sunday 12 noon to 10.30 pm.* ☎ *01283 703188*

Derbyshire

1 With your back to the pub turn right for no more than 200 yards. Immediately beyond house number 29 turn right along the path. Keep on the left side of the two fields beyond. A step-over stile leads to a footbridge over a brook. Stay on the path through the wood to reach a gate. Pass through this and keep forward, keeping just to the left of the electricity pylon ahead. This brings you to some high ground with good views. Cross another stile beside a gate. Head slightly right towards the left side of the woodland (**Church Spinney**) ahead. Then, with the spinney on your right, head across the field, with a church ahead, slightly right.

2 On reaching a track, turn left for 120 yards, then right, signed '**Foremarke Hall**'. (Please bear in mind that the footpath is passing through 'private grounds' – as you will see from the sign.) Pass a pond on your left, with the Hall on your right. Keep forward along the tarmac access road, following it round to the

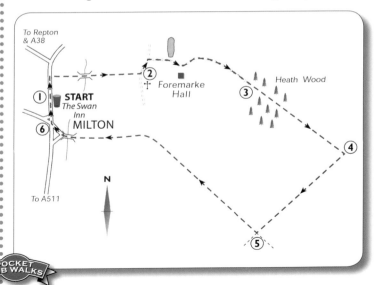

The imposing Foremarke Hall, built in 1760, is now a school.

right and then left in front of a long, low redbrick building. On reaching a small green keep to the right of it to walk on the left side of a tall brick wall. The track takes you into the countryside. Ignore all other tracks and paths to left and right. You begin to climb steadily and, ½ mile after leaving the properties in and around Foremarke Hall, you reach **Heath Wood**. Just before the wood look to your right. In the conifer trees in the field is a Danish barrow cemetery (according to the OS map) and you don't see many of them!

3 Follow the path up through the wood. At the top end of it continue forward between the trees ahead and squeeze out beside the gate onto a lane.

4 Turn right along the lane for about 200 yards.

Derbyshire

5 Turn right again onto the bridleway, which can be muddy. Keep in the same direction alongside three fields, looking out for **Hangman's Stone** on your left, 30 yards or so before the end of the third one. Turn right immediately you enter the fourth field, still on a bridleway. Eventually you join another track; ignore the track to the right here. Ahead you should be able to see the church spire in **Repton**. Ignore another track/bridleway to the left. Keep forward towards the cooling towers. Where the track you're on swings right and fizzles out keep forward beside a line of trees on your left. The bridleway then cuts through a wood. On the far side keep forward, with a hedge now on your left. Swing right at the end of the field, then left almost immediately between hedges. This brings you down between a couple of properties, where you should keep forward along the lane in front. Cross a brook and keep right.

6 On reaching the main road, turn right, back to the pub.

Places of interest nearby

This is easy – **Repton**! Just wander around the church, the market cross area and the main street. If you get a copy of the *Repton Trail*, then it will be even better. And you *must* go down into the Anglo-Saxon crypt – it's over 1,100 years old! (I found it rather spooky to be honest; so take someone with you and send them in first.) You can also see where the actor Basil Rathbone studied whilst you're in the town. All in all it's a fascinating place.

14 Swarkestone

The Crewe & Harpur Arms

There's one thing about walking just south of Derby – it will be flat. But that doesn't mean it's uninteresting. On 6th December 1745 Bonnie Prince Charlie ordered his men to head back to Scotland after 'invading' England. Swarkestone Bridge (in front of the pub) was as far south as they had reached. He had been hoping to claim the throne of England, to which he believed he was entitled. Swarkestone Bridge is reputedly the longest stone bridge in England. It's over three-quarters of a mile long, so this could be true. The walk takes you beside a section of what remains of the Derby Canal and you also stroll alongside the Trent & Mersey Canal, which is in much better condition. On the way back you'll catch a glimpse of the Pavilion, another ancient landmark, though no one knows for sure quite what its purpose was.

Distance – 3½ miles.

OS Explorer 245 The National Forest and 259 Derby. GR 369286.

This is a flat, leisurely, easy walk.

Starting point The car park of the Crewe & Harpur Arms (parking available for customers, with the landlord's permission).

How to get there Swarkestone is just under a mile south of Derby. Follow the A514 south for Ticknall. The Crewe & Harpur is on the right, just before Swarkestone Bridge.

THE PUB The food and beer at the **Crewe & Harpur Arms** are great. The menu is large, so you could find yourself tempted by a dish like lamb and dumplings or fruity chicken curry. If you fancy something lighter, then perhaps the Crewe and Harpur's 'Light Bites' might be the thing – Cajun chicken or a 5oz gammon or rump steak are a couple of these smaller meals. The regular ales are Marston's Pedigree and Banks's Bitter. Then there might be a seasonal beer like Rockin' Robin. There's been an inn on this site for over 800 years – though this one *only* dates back to 1744. It could probably tell a few tales.

Opening times 11 am to 11 pm every day.
☎ *01332 700641*

1 Stand with your back to the front of the pub, facing the **River Trent**. Turn right through the village of **Swarkestone**. You reach a crossroads.

2 Head straight across along **Lowes Lane**. Pass a nursery on your left. The lane passes over the **Trent & Mersey Canal**. Keep forward along the lane in front. Pass (what used to be) **Lowes Farm** on your left. Almost immediately on your right is one of the earthworks of **Swarkestone Lows** – ancient burial sites. Cross the bridge over the A50. Keep on the lane beyond as it bends slightly right, then left, ignoring tracks to the left. By now the lane will be a packed mud and stone track. This winds through the fields. At a T-junction of tracks, turn right, then cross a ditch, continuing forward towards a group of buildings. The tarmac lane you've reached swings right and almost immediately you're in a built-up area.

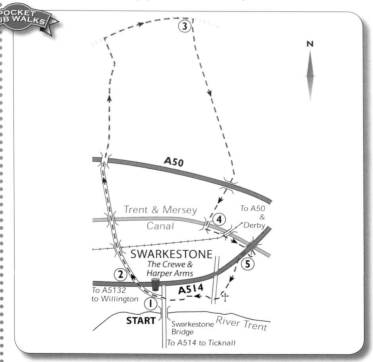

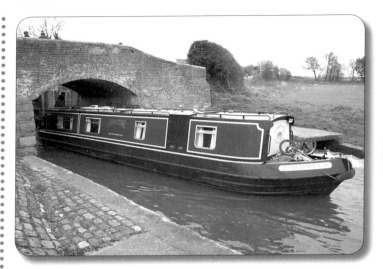

3 Before that though there's the **Derby Canal towpath**, known as the **Cloud Trail**. Turn right along the Trail, signed to **Swarkestone** and **Melbourne**. You then follow the Trail for nearly ½ mile. There's not much sign of a canal though. The Trail then bears right over a narrow bridge, part of the National Cycle Network no 6. This swings right, then left immediately, signed to **Melbourne** and **Leicester**. The Trail continues under the A50. At a redbrick bridge go left towards the **Trent & Mersey Canal** ahead.

4 Cross a bridge over the canal, with **Swarkestone Lock** on your right. Turn left, with the canal on your left. Pass under the railway bridge and then a low roadbridge. Keep right immediately beyond it to rise up to the road.

5 Turn left on the road for 200 yards. Pass through a gateway on your left, heading across the field for the church. Across the field to your left is the **Swarkestone Pavilion**, possibly a place

where wives of old could watch their husbands bowling on the green in front of it. Walk round to the main gate (between two yew trees) leading into the churchyard but don't enter it. Turn right to follow the path along a track, bearing left after 20 yards through a gap beside a gate. Walk directly away from the church (underneath the electricity lines) to follow the footpath beside a wall on your left. Stay on the path as it bears left and then right to lead you back to the **Crewe & Harpur Arms**.

Places of interest nearby

Head back into **Derby** and visit the **Museum and Art Gallery**, where there are some mummies and numerous other interesting items.
☎ *01332 716659*

Or you could visit **Derby cathedral** and look for the tomb of Bess of Hardwick who built Hardwick Hall (see walk 8).
☎ *01332 613576*

The Harrington Arms

The village of Thulston, on the south-eastern side of Derby, still has a country feel to it, though the city creeps ever nearer. Hopefully Thulston won't get swallowed up. The walk passes through the Elvaston Castle grounds, which have been extensively open to the public when owned by Derbyshire County Council. Whatever happens to the estate in the future, this walk should be OK, as it uses established rights of way, allowing continued access to this picturesque site.

THE PUB

There can't be many pubs that have a beer brewed especially for them but that's the case with the **Harrington Arms**. Wicked Hathern Brewery produces Earl of Harrington bitter just for this pub – and it wins awards. They also have Bass on offer as well as a couple of guests, something like Marston's Ashes Ale or Spitfire. There's plenty of choice foodwise, with home made steak and ale pie proving popular, also fresh fish, home made lasagne and filled baguettes, just to give you an idea. The staff are friendly and the pub has a good reputation. You can't ask more than that.

Opening times 11.30 am until 3 pm and 6 pm until 11 pm – the pub doesn't open Monday lunchtimes though.
☎ 01332 571798

1 With your back to the pub turn left along the main road through **Thulston**. Follow this, ignoring lanes to the right, to enter **Elvaston**. Ignore **Silver Lane** on your left and pass the

Distance – 3¼ miles.

OS Explorer 259 Derby. GR 408319.

Definitely the easiest walk in the book, more of a stroll if anything. I can't recall any effort being needed.

Starting point The Harrington Arms – either park in their car park (but let the landlord know) or on the street nearby.

How to get there Take the A6 south-eastwards from Derby and look out for the signs for Thulston and Elvaston. The Harrington Arms is on the outside of a right hand bend.

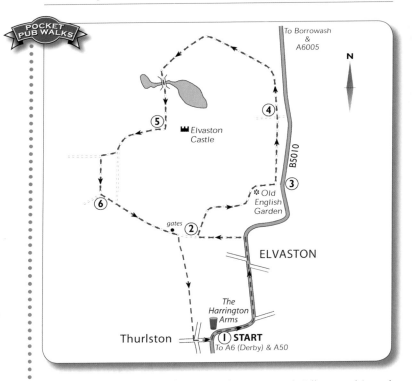

war memorial. Turn left along the tarmac bridleway (signed '**Elvaston Cricket Club**'), passing house number 15 on your left. Pass redbrick **Elvaston village hall**.

2 Some 150 yards beyond the redbrick village hall turn right along the gravel track. Stay on the bridleway as it bends right then left to reach the **Old English Garden** on your right. (At the time of writing you can look round this – and it is well worth it.) At the far end turn right. Within a few yards, the bridleway forks; take the left fork to reach another tarmac drive, where you bear right, with a hedge and woodland on your left.

3 Just 25 yards before the road turn left into the wood. Keep forward, then with the road on your right. On reaching a drive leading into **Elvaston Castle Country Park**, cross this and continue in the wood on the far side.

4 Follow the bridleway for a further 500 yards, keeping parallel to the road to your right. Cross another entrance as the bridleway bears left, away from the road. On your right there should be green fields. At a crossroads of tracks, go straight across, signed (at present) 'Park Centre & Castle'. Cross the north-western end of **The Lake**, continuing towards the castle buildings.

The unusual redbrick building in the grounds of Elvaston Castle.

Derbyshire

5 On reaching an unusual redbrick building on your right, turn right immediately along the tarmac driveway, passing through a pair of gateposts. Keep on the drive away from the castle (at present there is duckboarding at the side of the drive). Where the lane bears left, bear right to walk along a gravel bridleway into the open. You reach some riding paddocks on your left. Immediately after crossing a small redbrick bridge turn left alongside the paddocks.

6 On reaching a T-junction (with no public access to the right) turn left. You then join a tarmac drive coming in from the left. Keep forward along it. Ignore the left turn to **Elvaston church**. You then reach some impressive blue, red and gold gates on your left. Bear half right to pick up a footpath just to the left of a gate across a track. Pass through the wooden kissing gate and keep just to the left of a small wood jutting out into the field. The path should be visible on the ground. It's a long field; aim for the far left corner of it. Pass through another kissing gate and proceed beside the fence on your left. Pass through another kissing gate, heading forward through the paddock. You reach a crossroads, where you should keep forward towards the main road. The **Harrington Arms** is to your left.

Places of interest nearby

    Calke Abbey, a National Trust property, is a few miles south-west of Thulston, and well worth a visit. There's a lovely walled garden there and, in the words of the website, a 'stunning 18th-century Chinese silk bed'.
☎ *01332 863822*